FEELING IS THE SECRET

INCLUDES TWO BONUS LECTURES

YOU ARE A COSMIC BEING, WALK BY FAITH

Neville Goddard

The Milky Way Publications

ISBN: 978-81-979644-8-0

Publisher: The Milky Way Publications
Mumbai, Maharashtra

Phone: +91 9167080475
WhatsApp: +91 9167080475
E-mail: themilkywaypublications@gmail.com

First Edition: 2024

FEELING IS THE SECRET
Neville Goddard

CONTENTS

Foreword

THIS book is concerned with the art of realizing your desire. It gives you an account of the mechanism used in the production of the visible world. It is a small book but not slight. There is a treasure in it, a clearly defined road to the realization of your dreams.

Were it possible to carry conviction to another by means of reasoned arguments and detailed instances, this book would be many times its size. It is seldom possible, however, to do so by means of written statements or arguments since to the suspended judgment it always seems plausible to say that the author was dishonest or deluded, and, therefore, his evidence was tainted. Consequently, I have purposely omitted all arguments and testimonials, and simply challenge the open-minded reader to practice the law of consciousness as revealed in this book. Personal success will prove far more convincing than all the books that could be written on the subject. - NEVILLE

Feeling Is The Secret

Chapter One – Law and Its Operation

THE world, and all within it, is man's conditioned consciousness objectified. Consciousness is the cause as well as the substance of the entire world.

So it is to consciousness that we must turn if we would discover the secret of creation.

Knowledge of the law of consciousness and the method of operating this law will enable you to accomplish all you desire in life.

Armed with a working knowledge of this law, you can build and maintain an ideal world.

Consciousness is the one and only reality, not figuratively but actually. This reality may for the sake of clarity be likened unto a stream which is divided into two parts, the conscious and the subconscious. In order to intelligently operate the law of consciousness, it is necessary to understand the relationship between the conscious and the subconscious.

The conscious is personal and selective; the subconscious is impersonal and non-selective. The conscious is the realm of effect; the subconscious is the realm of cause. These two aspects are the male and female divisions of consciousness. The conscious is male; the subconscious is female.

The conscious generates ideas and impresses these ideas on the subconscious; the subconscious receives ideas and gives form and expression to them.

By this law - first conceiving an idea and then impressing the idea conceived on the subconscious - all things evolve out of consciousness; and without this sequence, there is not anything made that is made.

The conscious impresses the subconscious, while the subconscious expresses all that is impressed upon it.

The subconscious does not originate ideas, but accepts as true those which the conscious mind feels to be true and, in a way known only to itself, objectifies the accepted ideas.

Therefore, through his power to imagine and feel and his freedom to choose the idea he will entertain, man has control over creation. Control of the subconscious is accomplished through control of your ideas and feelings.

The mechanism of creation is hidden in the very depth of the subconscious, the female aspect or womb of creation.

The subconscious transcends reason and is independent of induction. It contemplates a feeling as a fact existing within itself and on this assumption proceeds to give expression to it. The creative process begins with an idea and its cycle runs its course as a feeling and ends in a volition to act.

Ideas are impressed on the subconscious through the medium of feeling.

No idea can be impressed on the subconscious until it is felt, but once felt - be it good, bad or indifferent - it must be expressed.

Feeling is the one and only medium through which ideas are conveyed to the subconscious.

Therefore, the man who does not control his feeling may easily impress the subconscious with undesirable states. By control of feeling is not meant restraint or suppression of your feeling, but rather the disciplining of self to imagine and entertain only such feeling as contributes to your happiness.

Control of your feeling is all important to a full and happy life.

Never entertain an undesirable feeling, nor think sympathetically about wrong in any shape or form. Do not dwell on the imperfection of yourself or others. To do so is to impress the subconscious with these limitations. What you do not want done unto you, do not feel that it is done unto you or another. This is the whole law of a full and happy life. Everything else is commentary.

Every feeling makes a subconscious impression and, unless it is counteracted by a more powerful feeling of an opposite nature, must be expressed.

The dominant of two feelings is the one expressed. I am healthy is a stronger feeling than I will be healthy. To feel I will be is to confess I am not; I am is stronger than I am not.

What you feel you are always dominates what you feel you would like to be; therefore, to be realized, the wish must be felt as a state that is rather than a state that is not Sensation precedes manifestation and is the foundation upon which all manifestation rests. Be careful of your moods and feelings, for there is an unbroken connection between your feelings and your visible world. Your body is an emotional filter and bears the unmistakable marks of your prevalent emotions. Emotional disturbances, especially suppressed emotions, are the causes of all disease. To feel intensely about a wrong without voicing or expressing that feeling is the beginning of disease - dis-ease - in both body and environment. Do not entertain the feeling of regret or failure for frustration or detachment from your objective results in disease.

Think feelingly only of the state you desire to realize. Feeling the reality of the state sought and living and acting on that conviction is the way of all seeming miracles. All changes of expression are brought about through a change of feeling. A change of feeling is a change of destiny. All creation occurs in the domain of the subconscious. What you must acquire, then, is a reflective control of the operation of the subconscious, that is, control of your ideas and feelings.

Chance or accident is not responsible for the things that happen to you, nor is predestined fate the author of your fortune or misfortune. Your subconscious impressions determine the conditions of your world. The subconscious is not selective; it is impersonal and no respecter of persons [Acts 10:34; Romans 2:11]. The subconscious is not concerned with the truth or falsity of your feeling. It always accepts as true that which you feel to be true. Feeling is the assent of the subconscious to the truth of that which is declared to be true. Because of this quality of the subconscious there is nothing impossible to man. Whatever the mind of man can conceive and feel as true, the subconscious can and must objectify. Your feelings create the pattern from which your world is fashioned, and a change of feeling is a change of pattern.

The subconscious never fails to express that which has been impressed upon it.

The moment it receives an impression, it begins to work out the ways of its expression. It accepts the feeling impressed upon it, your feeling, as a fact existing within itself and immediately sets about to produce in the outer or objective world the exact likeness of that feeling.

The subconscious never alters the accepted beliefs of man. It out-pictures them to the last detail whether or not they are beneficial.

To impress the subconscious with the desirable state, you must assume the feeling that would be yours had you already realized your wish. In defining your objective, you must be concerned only with the objective itself. The manner of expression or the difficulties involved are not to be considered by you. To think feelingly on any state impresses it on the subconscious. Therefore, if you dwell on difficulties, barriers or delay, the subconscious, by its very non-selective nature, accepts the feeling of difficulties and obstacles as your request and proceeds to produce them in your outer world.

The subconscious is the womb of creation. It receives the idea unto itself through the feelings of man. It never changes the idea received, but always gives it form. Hence the subconscious out-pictures the idea in the image and likeness of the feeling received. To feel a state as hopeless or impossible is to impress the subconscious with the idea of failure.

Although the subconscious faithfully serves man, it must not be inferred that the relation is that of a servant to a master as was anciently conceived. The ancient prophets called it the slave and servant of man. St. Paul personified it as a "woman" and said: "The woman should be subject to man in everything" [Ephesians 5:24; also, 1Corinthians 14:34, Ephesians 5:22, Colossians 3:18, 1Peter 3:1]. The subconscious does serve man and faithfully gives form to his feelings. However, the subconscious has a distinct distaste for compulsion and responds to persuasion rather than to command; consequently, it resembles the beloved wife more than the servant.

"The husband is head of the wife," Ephesians 5[:23], may not be true of man and woman in their earthly relationship, but it is true of the conscious and the subconscious, or the male and female aspects of consciousness. The mystery to which Paul referred when he wrote, "This is a great mystery [5:32]... He that loveth his wife loveth himself [5:28]... And they two shall be one flesh [5:31]", is simply the mystery of consciousness. Consciousness is really one and undivided but for creation's sake it appears to be divided into two.

The conscious (objective) or male aspect truly is the head and dominates the subconscious (subjective) or female aspect.

However, this leadership is not that of the tyrant, but of the lover.

So, by assuming the feeling that would be yours were you already in possession of your objective, the subconscious is moved to build the exact likeness of your assumption.

Your desires are not subconsciously accepted until you assume the feeling of their reality, for only through feeling is an idea subconsciously accepted and only through this subconscious acceptance is it ever expressed.

It is easier to ascribe your feeling to events in the world than to admit that the conditions of the world reflect your feeling. However, it is eternally true that the outside mirrors the inside.

"As within, so without" ["As above, so below; as below, so above; as within, so without; as without, so within",

"Correspondence", the second of The Seven Principles of Hermes Trismegistus].

"A man can receive nothing unless it is given him from heaven" [John 3:27] and "The kingdom of heaven is within you" [Luke 17:21]. Nothing comes from without; all things come from within
- from the subconscious.

It is impossible for you to see other than the contents of your consciousness. Your world in its every detail is your consciousness objectified. Objective states bear witness of subconscious impressions. A change of impression results in a change of expression.

The subconscious accepts as true that which you feel as true, and because creation is the result of subconscious impressions, you, by your feeling, determine creation.

You are already that which you want to be, and your refusal to believe this is the only reason you do not see it.

To seek on the outside for that which you do not feel you are is to seek in vain, for we never find that which we want; we find only that which we are.

In short, you express and have only that which you are conscious of being or possessing. "To him that hath it is given" [Matthew 13:12; 25:29; Mark 4:25; Luke 8:18; 19:26]. Denying the evidence of the senses and appropriating the feeling of the wish fulfilled is the way to the realization of your desire.

Mastery of self-control of your thoughts and feelings is

your highest achievement.

However, until perfect self-control is attained, so that, in spite of appearances, you feel all that you want to feel, use sleep and prayer to aid you in realizing your desired states.

These are the two gateways into the subconscious.

Chapter Two - Sleep

SLEEP, the life that occupies one-third of our stay on earth, is the natural door into the subconscious.

So it is with sleep that we are now concerned. The conscious two-thirds of our life on earth is measured by the degree of attention we give sleep. Our understanding of and delight in what sleep has to bestow will cause us, night after night, to set out for it as though we were keeping an appointment with a lover.

"In a dream, in a vision of the night, when deep sleep falleth upon men, in slumbering upon the bed; then he openeth the ears of men and sealeth their instruction", Job 33.

It is in sleep and in prayer, a state akin to sleep, that man enters the subconscious to make his impressions and receive his instructions. In these states the conscious and subconscious are creatively joined. The male and female become one flesh. Sleep is the time when the male or conscious mind turns from the world of sense to seek its lover or subconscious self.

The subconscious - unlike the woman of the world who marries her husband to change him - has no desire to change the conscious, waking state, but loves it as it is and faithfully reproduces its likeness in the outer world of form.

The conditions and events of your life are your children formed from the molds of your subconscious impressions in sleep. They are made in the image and likeness of your innermost feeling that they may reveal you to yourself.

"As in heaven, so on earth" [Matthew 6:10; Luke 11:2]. As in the subconscious, so on earth.

Whatever you have in consciousness as you go to sleep is the measure of your expression in the waking two-thirds of your life on earth.

Nothing stops you from realizing your objective save your failure to feel that you are already that which you wish to be, or that you are already in possession of the thing sought. Your subconscious gives form to your desires only when you feel your wish fulfilled.

The unconsciousness of sleep is the normal state of the subconscious. Because all things come from within yourself, and your conception of yourself determines that which comes, you should always feel the wish fulfilled before you drop off to sleep.

You never draw out of the deep of yourself that which you want; you always draw that which you are, and you are that which you feel yourself to be as well as that which you feel as true of others.

To be realized, then, the wish must be resolved into the feeling of being or having or witnessing the state sought. This is accomplished by assuming the feeling of the wish fulfilled. The feeling which comes in response to the question "How would I feel were my wish realized?" is the feeling which should monopolize and immobilize your attention as you relax into sleep. You must be in the consciousness of being or having that which you want to be or to have before you drop off to sleep.

Once asleep, man has no freedom of choice. His entire slumber is dominated by his last waking concept of self.

It follows, therefore, that he should always assume the feeling of accomplishment and satisfaction before he retires in sleep, "Come before me with singing and thanksgiving" [Psalm 95:2], "Enter into his gates with thanksgiving and into his courts with praise" [Psalm 100:4]. Your mood prior to sleep defines your state of consciousness as you enter into the presence of your everlasting lover, the subconscious.

She sees you exactly as you feel yourself to be. If, as you prepare for sleep, you assume and maintain the consciousness of success by feeling "I am successful", you must be successful. Lie flat on your back with your head on a level with your body. Feel as you would were you in possession of your wish and quietly relax into unconsciousness.

"He that keepeth Israel shall neither slumber nor sleep" [Psalm 121:4]. Nevertheless "He giveth his beloved sleep" [Psalm 127:2].

The subconscious never sleeps. Sleep is the door through which the conscious, waking mind passes to be creatively joined to the subconscious.

Sleep conceals the creative act, while the objective world reveals it.

In sleep, man impresses the subconscious with his conception of himself.

What more beautiful description of this romance of the conscious and subconscious is there than that told in the "Song of Solomon": "By night on my bed I sought him whom my soul loveth [3:1]... I found him whom my soul loveth; I held him and I not let him go, until I had brought him into my mother's house, and into the chamber of her that conceived me" [3:4].

Preparing to sleep, you feel yourself into the state of the answered wish, and then relax into unconsciousness. Your realized wish is he whom you seek. By night, on your bed, you seek the feeling of the wish fulfilled that you may take it with you into the chamber of her that conceived you, into sleep or the subconscious which gave you form, that this wish also may be given expression.

This is the way to discover and conduct your wishes into the subconscious. Feel yourself in the state of the realized wish and quietly drop off to sleep.

Night after night, you should assume the feeling of being, having and witnessing that which you seek to be, possess and see manifested. Never go to sleep feeling discouraged or dissatisfied. Never sleep in the consciousness of failure.

Your subconscious, whose natural state is sleep, sees you as you believe yourself to be, and whether it be good, bad or indifferent, the subconscious will faithfully embody your belief.

As you feel so do you impress her; and she, the perfect lover, gives form to these impressions and out-pictures them as the children of her beloved.

"Thou art all fair, my love; there is no spot in thee" [Song of Solomon 4:7] is the attitude of mind to adopt before dropping off to sleep.

Disregard appearances and feel that things are as you wish them to be, for "He calleth things that are not seen as though they were, and the unseen becomes seen" [Approx., Romans 4:17]. To assume the feeling of satisfaction is to call conditions into being which will mirror satisfaction.

"Signs follow, they do not precede".

Proof that you are will follow the consciousness that you are; it will not precede it.

You are an eternal dreamer dreaming non-eternal dreams. Your dreams take form as you assume the feeling of their reality.

Do not limit yourself to the past.

Knowing that nothing is impossible to consciousness, begin to imagine states beyond the experiences of the past.

Whatever the mind of man can imagine, man can

realize. All objective (visible) states were first subjective (invisible) states, and you called them into visible by assuming the feeling of their reality.

The creative process is first imagining and then believing the state imagined. Always imagine and expect the best.

The world cannot change until you change your conception of it. "As within, so without".

Nations, as well as people, are only what you believe them to be. No matter what the problem is, no matter where it is, no matter whom it concerns, you have no one to change but yourself, and you have neither opponent nor helper in bringing about the change within yourself. You have nothing to do but convince yourself of the truth of that which you desire to see manifested.

As soon as you succeed in convincing yourself of the reality of the state sought, results follow to confirm your fixed belief. You never suggest to another the state which you desire to see him express; instead, you convince yourself that he is already that which you desire him to be.

Realization of your wish is accomplished by assuming the feeling of the wish fulfilled. You cannot fail unless you fail to convince yourself of the reality of your wish. A change of belief is confirmed by a change of expression.

Every night, as you drop off to sleep, feel satisfied and spotless, for your subjective lover always forms the objective world in the image and likeness of your conception of it, the conception defined by your feeling.

The waking two-thirds of your life on earth ever corroborates or bears witness to your subconscious impressions. The actions and events of the day are effects; they are not causes. Free will is only freedom of choice.

"Choose ye this day whom ye shall serve" [Joshua 24:15] is your freedom to choose the kind of mood you assume; but the expression of the mood is the secret of the subconscious.

The subconscious receives impressions only through the feelings of man and, in a way known only to itself, gives these impressions form and expression.

The actions of man are determined by his subconscious impressions.

His illusion of free will, his belief in freedom of action, is but ignorance of the causes which make him act. He thinks himself free because he has forgotten the link between himself and the event.

Man awake is under compulsion to express his subconscious impressions. If in the past he unwisely impressed himself, then let him begin to change his thought and feeling, for only as he does so will he change his world. Do not waste one moment in regret, for to think feelingly of the mistakes of the past is to reinfect yourself. "Let the dead bury the dead" [Matthew 8:22; Luke 9:60]. Turn from appearances and assume the feeling that would be yours were you already the one you wish to be.

Feeling a state produces that state.

The part you play on the world's stage is determined by your conception of yourself.

By feeling your wish fulfilled and quietly relaxing into sleep, you cast yourself in a star role to be played on earth tomorrow, and, while asleep, you are rehearsed and instructed in your part.

The acceptance of the end automatically wills the means of realization. Make no mistake about this. If, as you prepare for sleep, you do not consciously feel yourself into the state of the answered wish, then you will take with you into the chamber of her who conceived you the sum total of the reactions and feelings of the waking day; and while asleep, you will be instructed in the manner in which they will be expressed tomorrow. You will rise believing that you are a free agent, not realizing that every action and event of the day is predetermined by your concept of self as you fell asleep. Your only freedom, then, is your freedom of reaction. You are free to choose how you feel and react to the day's drama, but the drama – the actions, events and circumstances of the day – have already been determined.

Unless you consciously and purposely define the attitude of mind with which you go to sleep, you unconsciously go to sleep in the composite attitude of mind made up of all feelings and reactions of the day. Every reaction makes a subconscious impression and, unless counteracted by an opposite and more dominant feeling, is the cause of future action.

Ideas enveloped in feeling are creative actions. Use your divine right wisely. Through your ability to think and feel, you have dominion over all creation.

While you are awake, you are a gardener selecting seed for your garden, but "Except a corn of wheat fall into the ground and die, it abideth alone; but if it die, it bringeth forth much fruit" [John 12:24]. Your conception of yourself as you fall asleep is the seed you drop into the ground of the subconscious. Dropping off to sleep feeling satisfied and happy compels conditions and events to appear in your world which confirm these attitudes of mind.

Sleep is the door into heaven. What you take in as a feeling you bring out as a condition, action, or object in space. So sleep in the feeling of the wish fulfilled.

Chapter Three – Prayer

PRAYER, like sleep, is also an entrance into the subconscious.

"When you pray, enter into your closet, and when you have shut your door, pray to your Father which is in secret and your Father which is in secret shall reward you openly" [Matthew 6:6].

Prayer is an illusion of sleep which diminishes the impression of the outer world and renders the mind more receptive to suggestion from within. The mind in prayer is in a state of relaxation and receptivity akin to the feeling attained just before dropping off to sleep.

Prayer is not so much what you ask for, as how you prepare for its reception. "Whatsoever things ye desire, when ye pray believe that you have received them, and ye shall have them" [Mark 11:24].

The only condition required is that you believe that your prayers are already realized.

Your prayer must be answered if you assume the feeling that would be yours were you already in possession of your objective. The moment you accept the wish as an accomplished fact, the subconscious finds means for its realization. To pray successfully then, you must yield to the wish, that is, feel the wish fulfilled.

The perfectly disciplined man is always in tune with the wish as an accomplished fact.

He knows that consciousness is the one and only reality, that ideas and feelings are facts of consciousness and are as real as objects in space; therefore he never entertains a feeling which does not contribute to his happiness, for feelings are the causes of the actions and circumstances of his life.

On the other hand, the undisciplined man finds it difficult to believe that which is denied by the senses and usually accepts or rejects solely on appearances of the senses. Because of this tendency to rely on the evidence of the senses, it is necessary to shut them out before starting to pray, before attempting to feel that which they deny. Whenever you are in the state of mind "I should like to, but I cannot", the harder you try, the less you are able to yield to the wish. You never attract that which you want, but always attract that which you are conscious of being.

Prayer is the art of assuming the feeling of being and having that which you want.

When the senses confirm the absence of your wish, all conscious effort to counteract this suggestion is futile and tends to intensify the suggestion.

Prayer is the art of yielding to the wish and not the forcing of the wish. Whenever your feeling is in conflict with your wish, feeling will be the victor. The dominant feeling invariably expresses itself. Prayer must be without effort. In attempting to fix an attitude of mind which is denied by the senses, effort is fatal.

To yield successfully to the wish as an accomplished fact, you must create a passive state, a kind of reverie or meditative reflection similar to the feeling which precedes sleep. In such a relaxed state, the mind is turned from the objective world and easily senses the reality of a subjective state. It is a state in which you are conscious and quite able to move or open your eyes but have no desire to do so. An easy way to create this passive state is to relax in a comfortable chair or on a bed. If on a bed, lie flat on your back with your head on a level with your body, close the eyes and imagine that you are sleepy. Feel – I am sleepy, so sleepy, so very sleepy.

In a little while, a faraway feeling accompanied by a general lassitude and loss of all desire to move envelops you. You feel a pleasant, comfortable rest and not inclined to alter your position, although under other circumstances you would not be at all comfortable. When this passive state is reached, imagine that you have realized your wish – not how it was realized, but simply the wish fulfilled. Imagine in picture form what you desire to achieve in life; then feel yourself as having already achieved it. Thoughts produce tiny little speech movements which may be heard in the passive state of prayer as pronouncements from without. However, this degree of passivity is not essential to the realization of your prayers. All that is necessary is to create a passive state and feel the wish fulfilled.

All you can possibly need or desire is already yours. You need no helper to give it to you; it is yours now. Call your desires into being by imagining and feeling your wish fulfilled. As the end is accepted, you become totally indifferent as to possible failure, for acceptance of the end wills the means to that end. When you emerge from the moment of prayer, it is as though you were shown the happy and successful end of a play although you were not shown how that end was achieved. However, having witnessed the end, regardless of any anticlimactic sequence, you remain calm and secure in the knowledge that the end has been perfectly defined.

Chapter Four – Feeling

"NOT by might, nor by power, but by my spirit, saith the Lord of hosts" [Zechariah 4:6]. Get into the spirit of the state desired by assuming the feeling that would be yours were you already the one you want to be. As you capture the feeling of the state sought, you are relieved of all effort to make it so, for it is already so. There is a definite feeling associated with every idea in the mind of man. Capture the feeling associated with your realized wish by assuming the feeling that would be yours were you already in possession of the thing you desire, and your wish will objectify itself.

Faith is feeling, "According to your faith (feeling) be it unto you" [Matthew 9:29]. You never attract that which you want, but always that which you are. As a man is, so does he see. "To him that hath it shall be given and to him that hath not it shall be taken away..." [Matthew 13:12; 25:29; Mark 4:25; Luke 8:18; 19:26]. That which you feel yourself to be, you are, and you are given that which you are. So assume the feeling that would be yours were you already in possession of your wish, and your wish must be realized.

"So God created man in his own image, in the image of God created he him" [Genesis 1:27]. "Let this mind be in you which was also in Christ Jesus, who being in the form of God, thought it not robbery to be equal with God" [Philippians 2:5,6]. You are that which you believe yourself to be.

Instead of believing in God or in Jesus – believe you are God or you are Jesus. "He that believeth on Me, the works that I do shall he do also" [John 14:12] should be "He that believes as I believe the works that I do shall he do also". Jesus found it not strange to do the works of God, because He believed Himself to be God. "I and My Father are one" [John 10:30]. It is natural to do the works of the one you believe yourself to be. So live in the feeling of being the one you want to be and that you shall be.

When a man believes in the value of the advice given him and applies it, he establishes within himself the reality of success.

YOU ARE A COSMIC BEING

Tonight I want you to think of Christ as a cosmic being who contains everyone within him. Having died for all, this one being is in all, and will rise in all. Only one being can rise, for only one being fell. Having deliberately destroyed his temple in the fall, God, (this one being) is rebuilding his temple out of the redeemed, in order for it to become something far greater than it was prior to its destruction. One being, containing all within him, fell into this world of death to become individualized as you, as me. That same being will rise in us all, individually: and when he does the divine name "Lord" will be conferred upon the individual in whom he rose.

In Paul's wonderful letter to the Corinthians, he tells us: "From now on I regard no one from the human point of view; even though I once regarded Christ from a human point of view, I regard him thus no longer." Why? Because Paul was led from tradition to self-discovery. While determined to destroy those who believed in a savior other than the one he was taught to believe in, Paul discovered that the Christ of whom they spoke was a pattern of salvation contained within every child born of woman. It was Paul who said: "When it pleased God to reveal himself in me, I conferred not with flesh and blood." The pattern unfolds in only one way, and Paul tried to describe how it unfolded in him. I cannot find the true detail by his description of it, but Paul does tell us to imitate God as dear children.

Now, in order to imitate anyone or anything, it must be seen or heard first. How can you imitate something you cannot see or hear? It is my purpose to tell you how to imitate God as a dear child, for imitation can only be accomplished by hearing what took place and believing it. Now, the question is asked: "How can men imitate him whom they have never heard, and how can men hear unless there is a preacher? And how can there be a preacher unless he is sent." Faith comes from what is heard, and what is heard comes by preaching Christ. If, when I tell you I came out from the Father, you will accept my words and believe I am telling you the truth, then you will set your hope fully upon this promise and its unfoldment in you.

I tell you: one being fell to become all, and one being is going to rise in all, as each is called according to His purpose. I was called in 1959. He may call you tonight, but each one of us will be called individually by the same being who is rising in all.

I cannot conceive of anything comparable to this, for unless we are born from above we remain in the world of death, turning the wheel of recurrence over and over again. I can assure you from what I know from my inner vision, that everyone will escape. God will not leave one section of himself in the world of death. He is one being who - containing all -fell into the world of death. That same being, rising in each, individually according to his purpose, rebuilds his temple out of the redeemed.

If you would imitate God as a dear child you must first have a pattern from which you may follow. This is true in all walks of life. There must be a mold into which molten metal is poured in order to form a casting. Jesus Christ is the mold which "Must be perfect as your heavenly Father is perfect." Perfection is a molten state into which you must be reduced. Your physical body, when it is burned, it is reduced to dust; so it cannot be this body that is reduced to a molten state. No. It is not your physical body, but your Spiritual body.

Christianity is based upon the claim that a certain series of events happened in which God revealed himself in action for the salvation of man. It hasn't a thing to do with any individual man on the outside. Paul's story, which preceded the gospels by twenty or twenty-five years, is not concerned with what happens to the individual between the cradle and the grave.

If the one called Jesus was a carpenter, a mason, a bricklayer, or a pimp, it would not concern Paul. He was only interested in what happened in an individual. Paul knew he had awakened from the dream of life, but could not share his experiences with others except in words. We are told that he spent his last days from morning to night discussing the kingdom of God and trying to persuade others concerning Jesus, and some believed while others disbelieved.

This is true in this world in which we live. When I tell of what happened to me, individually, my experiences are so unusual the average person will not accept them. They - still in the world of Caesar - are more concerned with how to make that extra dollar then they are in the eternal world of life.

Although this world of death is temporal, it will continue as though it is forever, until the individual hears the Word of God and responds with faith by setting his hope fully upon the grace that is coming to him at the revelation of Jesus Christ within him. That is where the one being, containing all of us, fell. It was a deliberate act, and necessary in order to expand beyond what He was prior to the fall. We did nothing wrong to warrant our fall; rather we desired to enter this world of death. We agreed to take upon ourselves these dead garments; to be enslaved by them and to overcome them. We did it in perfect confidence that He who contained us all, would redeem us all.

In the 32nd chapter of the Book of Deuteronomy we are told that: "He has set bounds to the people according to the number of the sons of God;" therefore, every child is a garment worn by a son of God, and God will not leave one of his sons in this world of death. Rather, every son will rise, individually, to the realization that he is God the Father, as it takes all of us to form that one being who is God and Father of all.

When I speak of Jesus Christ I do not mean a man, but a pattern. Like Paul, I no longer regard Christ from the human point of view. I once regarded him as such, but not any more. Now I see him as a pattern of salvation which began to unfold in me back in 1959 when I awoke in my skull. Until that moment in time I - like you - had no idea I was buried there; but, because it happened to me, I will now prophecy for you. A storm wind will possess you, and you will awaken within yourself to discover you are entombed in your skull, from which you will emerge. That will be your birth from above, of which John speaks, saying: "Unless you are born from above you cannot enter the kingdom of God." This kingdom is the new age spoken of as that age - as opposed to this age.

This is the age of death where everything begins and

ends, while that age is eternal life. Having overcome the world of death, Jesus Christ (the pattern) unfolds as you rise, victorious, into the world of eternal life; for you are the gods who came down, individualized yourselves in order to rise as the Lord, as there is no other being.

The world may condemn you if you are a thief by profession, but Paul doesn't. It matters little what happens to you individually between the cradle and the grave. But it matters much if, when you hear my story of salvation you believe it; for then you will break the shell and rise above all this worldly nonsense. Salvation's story was told to us as it was to them; but it did not benefit them because
- believing this world of death was real - they were more interested in achieving greater intellect and more wealth here; therefore, the story was not received with faith.

I read a story concerning Lord Russell who, although loving to be called "Lord," said: "I regard religion as a disease, born of fear. A source of untold misery to the human race." Well, I tell you it is not a disease, although I know there are numberless forms of interpretation of the great mystery.

Like Paul, I was taught that Christ was a man who came into the world and claimed he was the Messiah to save the world. But I tell you, Christianity is based upon the claim that a certain series of supernatural events happened, in which God revealed himself in action for the salvation of man. When I realized that these events spelled out the pattern man who was Christ, I knew there was no other.

It takes the many blows of the world to reduce us to that liquid, cosmic being who awakens in the grave. That grave is not in some cemetery, but in the skull from which a storm wind will awaken you. In the Jerusalem Talmud, there is a tradition that the Messiah was born in Bethlehem the night of the destruction of Jerusalem, and he was carried off by a storm wind. I tell you this is true.

When the storm wind possessed me I reverberated from head to foot. I felt as though my body was being shattered as I awoke. Expecting to see the same room I had retired in, I awoke to find myself in a tomb which I intuitively knew to be my skull. It was sealed, and when I rolled a stone away, I discovered that I could force my head into the opening found there. This I did and I came out of that skull as a child comes out of the womb of a woman; but this was the womb from above rather than the womb from below, for you must be born from above in order to inherit the kingdom of God. Then the entire imagery as told us in scripture surrounded me, witnessing the event.

It is written that the angel of the Lord said to those who were going to be witnesses: "Go and you will find him, for God is born this day in Bethlehem. Look for this sign, which is a babe wrapped in swaddling clothes, lying on the floor." The witnesses then went hastily and found the sign; but they could not see he who was having the experience because he was Spirit, and since God is Spirit, it was God who was born.

Although I could not be seen by mortal eye, my witnesses could not see me; but I could see them and their every thought was objective to me. Then the sign of my birth was carried away by a storm wind.

Now, knowing myself to be God, who is a father, I must have a son to bear witness to my fatherhood. Five months later God's son David stood before me and called me father and I fulfilled his promise. Then I returned to the limitation of my cross in order to share my experiences with you, my brothers, to encourage you to believe. I saw my only son who is God's only son.

That son is the personification of all the generations of men and their experiences, proving that the race is finished and the crown of righteousness is mine. I have played every lovely and unlovely part in this world. I had to in order to see my son, whose beauty is beyond measure, and whose name is David.

Now, the third mighty act reveals your true identity as that of molten gold. In the Book of Zechariah, we read: "He stood upon the Mount of Olives when it was split from east to west as one half moved northward and the other half moved southward." You will discover, as I did, that the Mount of Olives spoken of here is your body; for the Old Testament is an adumbration, a forecasting in a not altogether conclusive and immediately evident way.

It is a shadow, but not the substance. Zechariah refers to a mountain, but when it happens to you, you will realize that the mountain is yourself. It is your body which is split from top to bottom, from east to west, as one side moves northward as the other side moves southward, revealing liquid, molten gold at its base. As I looked at this living, liquid gold I knew it to be myself; and I fused with it and up I went into my skull - into the kingdom of heaven, for the kingdom is within, At that moment I departed the world of generation and returned to the world of regeneration, as the heavens reverberated like thunder. Having returned to the molten state, I cast myself into the mold which was prepared for me before that the world was, to become the living image that radiates and reflects God's glory. I am now the express image of God Himself. God's primal wish was, "Let us make man in our image."

I tell you, He has wrought it! As one of the gods, I have completed the journey; but because we are all brothers, I am compelled to remain in the world to tell you in the hope that you who are still asleep will believe me. I say the Christ of scripture is a pattern of salvation and not a man separate from yourself.

The four mighty acts which form that redemption begin with your awakening within yourself and end with the descent of the dove. Two years and nine months after my ascent into the kingdom of heaven, the Holy Spirit descended upon me in bodily form as a dove and smothered me with love. Then I knew I had filled the entire role and was now a glorious, living stone in the living body of the Risen Christ.

Christ is the one being who fell containing all within himself. He chose us in him before the foundation of the world. Because he could not fall without all of us, we agreed to fall with him. That was an agreement for expansion, for truth is an ever expanding illumination. God, having reached the limit of contraction and opacity, died in order to rise into limitless expansion and translucency.

Opacity (which is doubt) is personified as a thing and called the devil; and this being called "man," is the limit of contraction. It may be hard to believe, but - as Paul said after his revelation: "The wisdom of this world is foolish in the eyes of God, and the foolishness of God is wiser than men and the weakness of God is stronger then men." Man believes he is getting wiser and wiser, yet it is only wiser and wiser nonsense. But God allows the nonsense to go on as men give each other medals, knowing that after the revelation man will know that the Bible is not speaking of a messiah to come from without, but from within.

One man fell, saying: "I say, You are gods, Sons of the Most High, all of you. Nevertheless you will fall like men and die as one man, O princes." Can you imagine that? Falling as one man we are princes; and if that is true, then our father is a king. I tell you, our Father is the King of kings and the Lord of lords, for he is the Lord God Jehovah who is raising us to himself that each one of us may become fully aware of being the Father. Regardless of your present sex, you are a son of Sod destined to awaken as the Father.

This wonderful story of scripture is completely misunderstood. Today's preachers are not sent, for they have not yet been awakened; therefore they will give you all kinds of stories concerning the interpretation of scripture. Prior to 1959 I was not sent, but in 1959 1 was called, incorporated into the body of God and sent. This incorporation is like an impression made by a seal on wax or clay, for I came out bearing the image of God. The mortal eye cannot see that image, and when I die here, my physical body will disintegrate like all bodies do. My friends will say I am dead, for to them I am a mortal being with weaknesses and limitations of the flesh.

Those who see me as Neville are misled, as they cannot

hear what I am saying; for they are seeing a body disintegrating before their eyes. They are judging by appearances and cannot understand that God does not see as man sees. Man sees the outward man, while God sees the inner man; and I, the inner man, have been impressed upon God like a great seal upon wax. I wear this little body that continues to decay; yet I, unseen by mortal eye, am radiating and reflecting the glory of God. I am the express image of the person that is God, but only those whose eyes are open will see me.

I promise you who hear me tonight, that it won't be long before you will depart this world. Don't be afraid. You will be restored to life, in a world just like this, to continue your journey. If you believe what you have heard from me, although I will not be there, wherever you go they will talk of the work I did here. Individually, I have left the world of death. I am only waiting for the moment when this little garment is taken off for the last time. I will not be restored to a world of mortality like this any more, for I have finished the race; I have fought the good fight; I have kept the faith. Now there is laid up for me the crown of righteousness where I go to wait for all my brothers to come into that union and be the one being that came down bearing all.

Mark my words, I am not fooling you. It isn't long to wait before you will take off this garment and find yourself restored to life. You will meet many of your friends there who went before you. It will be a world just like this, where you will do all of the things we do here. And you will remember who taught you. You will not see me there, but eventually you will see me. Now I am going to where you cannot come; but you will, for everyone will awaken as God the Father.

I am not trying to persuade you to change your attitude towards the speaker. I am only telling you what I know from experience. Like Paul, I did not receive this knowledge from a man; it came through revelation of the true nature of salvation. It's something entirely different. Salvation is not a man, but a pattern man buried in all, who will awaken in all in a first-person, singular, present-tense experience. When the experience is yours, you, too, will know who you are. I was taught to believe God was another; but when the pattern awakened in me, I knew I was He. Now I remain in the world only to share this wisdom with my brothers.

The unknown author of the Book of Hebrews said: "Holy brethren, look to Jesus, the apostle and high priest of our confession." We are all sharers in this great gift, so let us now look to Jesus, the apostle who is called and sent. It is Jesus who is called. That's who you really are. As the apostle, you are called and sent to tell the story of salvation from experience. You will tell your good news, knowing that not everyone who hears it will respond. In fact many, being more interested in the honors of men, will discount it.

Those who have $50 million are only interested in increasing their wealth to $100 million; and, although they may be eighty when they hear your story, it will not interest them, as they will still want more of what they must leave behind when they depart this world - as they won't be able to take it with them, as you know. They will make a world like this, only devoid of what they had built up here, and cast themselves in a role best suited for the work yet to be done in them by the son of God who is wearing that garment. He may zap him from the role of a millionaire and place him in the role of a shoe-shine boy or one who cleans latrines, if that is necessary for the work yet to be done in him.

The world into which they go is just as real as this. I know this is true from experience. I have sat in a chair and felt something happen within me and I see a world that is solidly real. As my consciousness follows vision, I step into that world and it closes upon me as this world is shut out. While in that world my body is real. It is seen and heard by others. If, in that world I have a body like this, yet those who are here see my body asleep in a chair, how did I get that body? It was just as real to me and to those who saw and heard me there as this body you now see here. You could destroy this body, but you would not have destroyed that body in that world.

William Blake once said: "The oak is cut down with the ax and the lamb is slain by the knife, but their forms eternal remain forever and are reproduced by the seed of contemplative thought." When I stepped into that world I knew myself to be a man called Neville. I was so aware of being Neville I clothed myself in the body that was Neville; yet I knew there was a body that was Neville, sound asleep on a chair.

How did it happen? By the seed of contemplative thought. When you die here, you remold yourself in the likeness that you know - only you reduce it in age to a time that pleases you. An eighty-year-old man, knowing what he knows now, will wear a twenty year old body, produced by the seed of contemplative thought. Who does it? The God in him. He will not go through the womb of a woman, but will create a new body by the seed of contemplative thought. He goes on in that world, just as he does here, to die there and begin all over again until he hears the story of salvation and believes.

Now let us go into the silence.

WALK BY FAITH

Blake asked the question: "Why is it that the Bible is more entertaining and instructive than any other book? Is it not because it is addressed to the Imagination, which is spiritual sensation, and only immediately to the understanding, or reason?"

The one book, called the Bible, is composed of sixty-six books. Take this challenge. Read each book as though the depth of your soul is speaking to your surface mind. As though the ineffable Imagination is speaking to the human Imagination, and not to your immediate understanding or reasoning mind.

Let us examine this thought. In his 2nd letter to the Corinthians Paul says: "We walk by faith and not by sight." When we walk by sight, we know our way by objects that the eye sees. But Paul tells us to order our life by objects seen only in the imagination. In other words, when you know where you want to go and what you want to be, you are told not to rearrange your physical structure, but to walk by faith, viewing only the rearranged structure of your mind. And if you will remain faithful to that state of consciousness, what is seen only in your imagination will objectify itself in your world.

Paul now adds another observation, saying: "This one thing I do. Forgetting what lies behind, I strain forward to what lies ahead." Paul's goal was the high calling of

God in Christ Jesus, but you need not have such a goal. Your desire could be a successful business. Now, everything begins in the imagination, for man is all imagination and God is man. God and man differ only in the degree of imagination's intensity. Now keyed low, man walks by sight or by faith in his human imagination. Walking by sight is easier, because buildings rarely move. But when you walk by faith, the objects in your mind's eye must remain as stable as those of the physical eye.

My brother Victor wanted to be a successful business man, and he knew how to remain faithful to what he imagined. In 1924, when our family didn't have a cent, Victor rearranged the name on a building (in his mind's eye) to imply we owned it. This he did for two years, when - without any more money than when he started imagining - a casual acquaintance purchased the building for us without collateral for $50,000. Eight years ago we sold the building to a bank for $850,000, and there is no capital gains tax in Barbados!

Walking by faith, every day as Victor passed that building, he saw "J. C. Goddard and Sons" on the marquee in place of the existing name of "I. N. Roach & Company". Sight told him the building belonged to another, but faith said the building was his. By simply rearranging the structure of his mind every day for two years, our family's fortune changed.

Now, we are told: "Faith is the assurance of things hoped for; the conviction of things not seen, so that what is seen was made out of things that do not appear." (Hebrews 11) Only my brother Victor saw his mental act. Others saw the sign, "J. N. Roach & Company"
- by sight, but Victor saw the words, "J.C. Goddard &

Sons" - by faith.

Someone once asked Blake what he saw when he looked at the sun, and he replied, "I see a host of angels singing, 'Holy, Holy, Holy, Lord God Almighty.'" We can all see the same tree but see it differently, just as we can the same man. One may see him in need, while another sees him gainfully employed, both using the same power. You have the power to either live by faith or by sight. If you live by sight, accepting everything that happens, you remain an automaton, unable to change the conditions and events in your world. Only as you begin to live by faith will your life change.

Paul tells us that no matter what he has done or did not do, he puts it behind him and stretches forward towards what lies ahead. Paul's ideal was to be called to the highest point of God. I hope this is your ideal, too, but perhaps it is not. Maybe other things are pressing upon you, such as the need for money. If so, make that your objective, but use the same technique.

Put the past behind you. Do not look back and become like Lot's wife who turned into a pillar of salt - which is a preservative. You always put what you want to preserve in brine. If you turn back and dwell upon the state you want to leave behind, you have placed it in brine and will become it once more. But if you will turn your back upon the past regardless of what you have or have not done, and stretch forward to what you want to be or do and remain faithful to your desire - nothing can stop you from achieving it. You will become the man you assume you are, if you persist in the assumption that you are already there!

Like Blake, I have found the Bible most entertaining,

challenging, and instructive. It is not an easy book to read, however. If it were, it would not be worth my care, for as the ancients discovered, that which is not too explicit is fittest for instruction, as it rouses the faculties to act.

Take this simple statement in Hebrews: "In many and various ways God spoke of old to our fathers by the prophets, but in these last days he has spoken to us by his son who reflects the glory of God and bears the stamp of his nature."

The prophets, instruments through which God spoke, recorded their visions of what God intended, saying: "The heavens declare the glory of God and the firmament shows forth his handiwork." (Psalms 18 & 19) But in the last days God speaks to us by his son, David. This is a fantastic revelation, for in the end God is going to reveal himself.

I could tell you until the ends of time that you are He, but only David can make you believe it. I'll tell you why. Many people, like Bishop Pike, question the authority of scripture; but it will never be questioned after it is experienced.

In the Book of Revelation, Jesus Christ is called "the word of God". And in the Book of John he declares his word is truth. May I tell you: only when a truth is experienced can it be known. I know what I have experienced is true. You have heard my words and believe me, but you will not know their truth to the degree that I do until they are experienced.

I have told you how my brother walked by faith rather than by sight, and created a fabulous business in the islands. Sight told him he didn't have a penny to his name. But in faith he began to alter his life by that which only his imagination could see. Your sight registers what is before you right now. If you do not like it, you have an "I" within that is Christ in you. He is the power of imagination which, through faith, can change your life.

As the operant power of your imagination, you can tell where you are going and what you are doing by watching your thoughts. If certain events in your past are unlovely and you remember them, you are ordering their experience. But if you turn your back on the past by forgetting what lies behind and stretch forward to what lies ahead, you will order your conversations aright and become what you behold. This truth will never be disproved, but you are its operant power and must live by it. You need nothing on the outside, but can start just where you are; but you must walk in the direction you set up in your imagination.

Ask yourself this simple question: What would it be like if it were true that I am now the person I want to be? Then reach for its feeling, its spiritual sensation. What is that? I'll show you in a very simple way. Feel a piece of glass, now feel a baseball. Does the baseball feel like glass? Can you feel a tennis ball? Does it feel like a baseball or a piece of glass? Can you feel a piece of cloth, a violet, a piano? Do they all feel alike? Of course not. That's spiritual sensation - a vivid way of seeing, hearing, smelling, tasting, and feeling reality.

A few years ago I gave a similar lecture in New York City and a lady in my audience decided to test me. While sitting in her chair she embraced a large bunch of roses. She smelled them, felt their velvety petals, and saw their beauty in her mind's eye. Then, breaking the silence she left my meeting and returned to her hotel room at the Waldorf Astoria.

The next day the queen mother, Queen Elizabeth, was given a party at the Waldorf Astoria, with two thousand people in attendance. After the reception the maitre d', not wanting to discard the flowers there, instructed his men to take three dozen roses up to this lady's room. And when she came home that evening, all she could smell were those lovely roses. She had embraced and lost herself in the feeling of the possession of beautiful roses. She walked by faith and not by sight, and the next day her room was filled with the heavenly aroma of roses.

Now, perhaps because of its memory, you find yourself continuing to look back at what you were (and are) and not ahead into what you want to be. If you will order your conversations aright, right now, their truth will happen in the simplest way.

A seamstress and dress designer I know wanted more money. Using her imagination, she held an envelope in her hand and listened to the paper tear as she opened it. Shaking the contents out, she counted the money to the very penny. This she did for seven nights. On the eighth day, a lady called, offering her a job which paid her, to the penny, what she had imagined. Do you know - that lady could have counted out much more and she would have received it, but she was quite satisfied with the amount she had imagined.

Now, if there is evidence for a thing, does it matter what the world thinks? Could you ever take this lady's experience from her? No! The truth, experienced by her parallels scripture, for all things are possible to one who believes. How did this lady believe what she was imagining? She did it by bringing forth all of her senses to bear upon this event. Using her sense of hearing, she heard the paper tear. Shaking the contents of the envelope, she heard the money fall on the table. She felt the envelope and saw the bills inside. Do you know, money has an odor unlike anything else? So you can smell money. She determined what she would do if she had the money and she did it.

Another lady went to Sterns Department Store in New York City, saying to herself: "Neville says I can have anything I want if I will imagine and believe in my imaginal act." Having no money, this lady walked over to the hat department, took off her hat and tried on a new one. Walking around the area, she admired herself in front of all the mirrors, but when she returned, her hat was gone. When she described it to the sales lady, she learned that her hat had been sold! The section manager was called in, and he told her to take any hat she wanted, compliments of Sterns. She liked the one she had been wearing, so she left the store with her new hat on her head, and she hadn't paid a dime for it.

Here is another story of a similar nature. This lady's profession was that of being a lady of the evening. She attended all of my meetings, and one day she said to me; "You know, Neville, the strangest thing happened. You told me that I could have anything I wanted if I simply imagined it.

One day I saw a beautiful hat in the window of a department store on Broadway. It was $18, but I loved it so I imagined wearing the hat. As I walked up the street I kept looking at my reflection in the shop windows, seeing that hat on my head. Arriving home, I imagined placing the new hat in the closet instead of my old one. Every day, for the next week or ten days, as I put on my old hat, I imagined it was the new one. Then one day a friend called and asked me to come see her. While there, she brought out a hat box and said; 'I must have been insane when I bought this hat. I wouldn't wear it to a dog fight; yet strangely enough I feel it would look lovely on you.' She opened the box and brought out, not a hat, but the hat, the very hat I had seen in the window and worn in my imagination." Then she asked: "Neville, why didn't God give me the money to buy the hat myself, instead of giving it to me in this manner?"

Knowing her profession, I said, "Ann, do you owe any rent?" and she replied, "Yes, two weeks." "What do you pay, about $17.50 per week?" "Yes." "So you owe $35. What price hats do you usually buy? Three or four dollar ones? Have you ever bought a $17 hat?" "Never." "Then tell me honestly. If, when you were looking at the hat, you had seen a $100 bill on the ground, would you have brought the hat?" She said "No." Then I said, "No matter how much money God might have given you, you still would not have bought the hat, so someone else had to buy it for you, and they did."

I have bought clothes, brought them home, and wondered what possessed me to buy them. I did it because someone was treading in the winepress elsewhere. Someone imagined a suit of clothes, so I went to my tailor, chose the cloth, and paid for the suit. But when I brought it home, my wife wouldn't let me bring it into the house. Then a friend who wanted something just like it contacted me and got the suit. He was treading the winepress while I paid for the suit.

Believe me, imagination is spiritual sensation. It is a vivid sight, a vivid sound. When Beethoven went deaf, all sound to the outer ear came to its end. Then Beethoven began to hear with the inner ear and wrote all of the beautiful music we so enjoy.

You can now think of someone you love and hear him speak. If you can't hear him, use one of your other spiritual senses. A touch, a sound, a sight, or an odor will do. I know in New York City, years ago, as I walked through Harlem, I smelled the odor of cooking that instantly took me to Barbados. Although I was physically in Harlem, my sense of smell told me I was 2000 miles away in Barbados.

You can remember a sound, a touch, a sight, and put yourself any place. Like Paul, learn to walk by faith and not by sight. Forget what lies behind and stretch forward to what lies ahead. In the third chapter of Philippians, Paul names his desire as the calling of God in Christ Jesus, but it need not be yours.

I urge you to try this, for your life is forever. Nothing dies. The little rose that blooms once blooms forever, for nothing passes away. If a loved one ceases to be in this little sphere he doesn't die, but is instantly restored to life to carry on his wonderful journey in this age until that moment in time when God speaks to him through his Son, who calls him Father. Only then will he know he is the author of his world. Then his journey will be over, and when he takes off his little garment it will be for the last time.

Paul tells us in Philippians; "I desire to depart and be

with Christ, for that is better by far, but it is more necessary that I remain in the flesh on your account." Paul longed to depart and be one with God the Father, but he knew it was necessary for him to remain in the flesh and continue his instruction, just as I do.

Take my words to heart and achieve your every desire. Learn to walk by faith and not by sight and, like Paul, turn your back upon everything you have ever accomplished and go forward - by faith - towards the goal you have set for yourself. Knowing what you would see if your goal were reached, how you would feel if you were there, what you would do now if it were true? Walk in that state and you will achieve it.

Now let us go into the silence.

www.ingramcontent.com/pod-product-compliance
Lightning Source LLC
Chambersburg PA
CBHW050026170726
48282CB00025B/559
9788197964480